MINIMALISM

How To Live A Meaningful Life With A Minimalist Lifestyle. Design Your Life With More Of Less

Descrierea CIP a Bibliotecii Naţionale a României
MILLBURN, CARY

    Minimalism. How To Live A Meaningful Life With A Minimalist Lifestyle. Design Your Life With More Of Les / by Cary Millburn. - Bucureşti : My Ebook, 2018
    ISBN 978-606-983-597-5

159.9

MINIMALISM

HOW TO LIVE A MEANINGFUL LIFE WITH A MINIMALIST LIFESTYLE. DESIGN YOUR LIFE WITH MORE OF LESS

My Ebook Publishing House
Bucharest, 2018

CONTENTS

Chapter 1. WHAT IS MINIMALISM 11
Chapter 2. CHOOSING A THEME 16
Chapter 3. FOCUSING ON A SPECIFIC AREA THAT GIVES YOU THE SENSES OF ACCOMPLISHMENT 21
Chapter 4. PICKING WHAT STAYS AND WHAT GOES 27
Chapter 5. PURCHASING BETTER 36
Chapter 6. FOLLOWING UP PERIODICALLY 40
Chapter 7. THE BENEFITS OF MINIMALISM 44
Conclusion 49

INTRODUCTION

A big thanks and congratulations for buying the book, **"Minimalism: How To Live A Meaningful Life With A Minimalist Lifestyle. Design Your Life With More Of Less"**

This book contains practical information about our reality lives at a hot pace. We are excessively rushed, excessively surged, and excessively focused. We work long, energetic hours to pay the bills, yet fall further into obligation. We surge starting with one action then onto the next – multitasking en route – yet never appear to complete everything. We stay in consistent association with others through our phones, however evident groundbreaking connections keep on eluding us.

Minimalism backs off life and liberates us from this cutting edge agitation to live quicker. It discovers opportunity to separate. It tries to keep just the basics. It tries to evacuate the trivial and keep the noteworthy. Furthermore, in doing as such, it esteems the purposeful undertakings that enhance life.

Thanks again for purchasing this book, I hope you enjoy it!

☐ Copyright 2018 by My Ebook Publishing House – All rights reserved

This document is geared towards providing exact and reliable information in regards to the topic and issue covered. The publication is sold with the idea that the publisher is not required to render accounting, officially permitted, or otherwise, qualified services. If advice is necessary, legal or professional, a practiced individual in the profession should be ordered.

– From a Declaration of Principles which was accepted and approved equally by a Committee of the American Bar Association and a Committee of Publishers and Associations.

In no way is it legal to reproduce, duplicate, or transmit any part of this document in either electronic means or in printed format. Recording of this publication is strictly prohibited and any storage of this document is not allowed unless with written permission from the publisher. All rights reserved.

The information provided herein is stated to be truthful and consistent, in that any liability, in terms of inattention or otherwise, by any usage or abuse of any policies, processes, or directions contained within is the solitary and utter responsibility of the recipient reader. Under no circumstances will any legal responsibility or blame be held against the publisher for any reparation, damages, or monetary loss due to the information herein, either directly or indirectly.

Respective authors own all copyrights not held by the publisher.

The information herein is offered for informational purposes solely, and is universal as so. The presentation of the information is without contract or any type of guarantee assurance.

The trademarks that are used are without any consent, and the publication of the trademark is without permission or backing by the trademark owner. All trademarks and brands within this book are for clarifying purposes only and are the owned by the owners themselves, not affiliated with this document.

CHAPTER ONE
WHAT IS MINIMALISM

We may characterize minimalism as clearing out excessive Junk. When you begin to unclutter, you instantly observe the advantages of living with less. This benefit might be something as straightforward as continually having the capacity to locate that one thing you used to invest energy searching for.

As you begin the advantage, you search for approaches to living more unprejudiced. What starts as an extreme adventure (giving things away, cutting the link), turns out to be extremely individual, deliberate and more significant. You begin to consider "stuff" not simply things but rather commitment, obligation, and stress. At that point, you perceive how this "stuff" is impeding your LIFE and choose to roll out a more significant improvement. It's now that minimalism turns out to be more about your identity, rather than what you have.

Modern culture has gotten tied up with the lie that the high life is found in aggregating things– in having however much as could be expected. They trust that more is better and have accidentally bought into the possibility that joy can be acquired at a retail establishment.

Be that as it may, they are incorrect. Minimalism brings opportunity from the all-devouring energy to have. It ventures off the treadmill of consumerism and sets out to look for satisfaction somewhere else. It esteems connections, encounters, and soul-mind. What's more, in doing as such, it discovers life.

Our reality lives at a hot pace. We are excessively rushed, excessively surged, and overly pushed. We work long, energetic hours to pay the bills, however, fall further into an obligation. We swell starting with one action then onto the next– multitasking en-route, yet never appear to complete everything. We stay in steady association with others through our PDAs. However obvious groundbreaking connections keep on eluding us.

Minimalism backs off life and liberates us from this advanced craziness to live speedier. It discovers an opportunity to withdraw. It tries to keep just the basics. It seeks to expel the paltry and prevent the huge. What's more, in doing as such, it esteems the deliberate undertakings that increase the value of life.

In spite of the fact that minimalism has turned out to be usually connected with feel, minimalism goes a long way past style and stylistic layout– the thought our lives could improve by living negligibly which can help any individual who's looking to de-mess their lives-be it a relationship or a closet. There are no particular rules on the moderate approach. It's exceptionally subjective since the point is to disentangle in a way that conveys productivity and bliss to the person. In spite of the fact that, there are some approaches to start and encourage the procedure.

We are always being *assaulted* by notices on TV, on the radio, on announcements, on YouTube, on sites, among different sources. Wherever we go, there are messages relating to us that we ought to spend more, purchase that item since it will improve us and that our motivation in life ought to be to amass more "stuff" that we don't require keeping in mind the end goal to live. It is troublesome for us to dismiss these messages since they are exploiting our natural human feelings and sentiments (like satisfaction, the dread of passing up a great opportunity, feeling sufficient, feeling fantastic, views of energy and distinction, emotions of worth and achievement, and so forth.).

Having more "stuff" and an excessive number of time responsibilities makes more pressure and hastiness in our lives, and these "things" take away our chance, vitality, and cash which could be spent seeking after more essential things throughout everyday life. We invest energy inquiring about our stuff before we buy, procuring the money to get them, and we invest time repairing, keeping up, and sorting out our stuff.

In case you're occupied with recovering your opportunity, having more vitality and sparing more cash, at that point continue perusing! Minimalism may be the change you require in your life.

So where do you begin on the way to minimalism?

CHAPTER TWO
CHOOSING A THEME

Ebbing to the point of style, numerous individuals do lean toward picking a subject to stick to when moving toward minimalism and this is not the slightest bit required. Choosing a specific theme can help the procedure since it makes it straightforward what to keep and what to dispose of or redistribute. A subject may likewise be all the more tastefully satisfying for a few. There are different manners by which the improvement can be drawn closer. If you do choose to run with a subject, pick something that you appreciate.

Would you like more joy and less pressure? Need to clean up for good? Do you battle with segregating your feelings from your stuff? Envision having a want for less stuff, not so much mess but slightly more time to appreciate the things that are imperative to you. Regardless of whether that is investing energy with family and companions, seeking after your most loved leisure or finding fulfilling work. In their lies:

- ❖ How and why we gather so much stuff
- ❖ How society impacts our shopping propensities
- ❖ What we should do to carry on with an enthusiasm filled life
- ❖ How to separate our feelings from our material?
- ❖ How to clean up
- ❖ How to frame and keep up a moderate attitude
- ❖ How to streamline our objectives and connections?

❖ How to end up plainly a recognizing buyer, and more!

Our lives have turned out to be so rushed. We are caught up with working endless hours so we can purchase more stuff to pack into our officially flooding houses. We wildly surge starting with one movement then onto the next without genuinely completing anything. We are continually connected to our cell phones, however, do not have any specific relationship development. We have turned out to be thoughtless robots driven by consumerism with the voracious need to obtain more things. Picking minimalism conflicts with every single mainstream tradition. Our general public is so charmed with material belonging and filling our timetables with apparently essential assignments that the choice to strip our lives to its uncovered segments appears to be absurd to a few people. Some way or another taking out the overabundance conveys peace and happiness to our lives. It enables us to concentrate on what is extremely imperative. Envision getting back home each day to a house loaded with space with everything in its place. Opening each storage room and bureau and adoring everything that is in it and knowing everything has exploitation and a reason. Looking at your timetable and anticipating each movement penciled in with the general population you appreciate. Envision more opportunity to go through with your companions, family and seeking your interests and things that are imperative to you. Consider being content with less. Envision never again feeling discontent with your life yet instead living every day for a genuine reason. Minimalism can enable you to concentrate on who you indeed are, your fantasies and interests and uncover your real self. When we dispose of the physical and mental mess, we are allowed to investigate life and all it brings to the table. It is conceivable to change your psyche and just want the things you need and lack.

Once that happens you will encounter genuine satisfaction.

Minimalists trust that there is something else entirely to live than collecting more stuff, burning through cash on things we don't need and filling our lives with time duties that we aren't enthusiastic about just to stay "occupied."

Minimalism is tied in with living a purposeful, essential and satisfying life through settling on conscious decisions. It implies less mess, fewer time responsibilities, less pressure, nervousness and belonging; additional time, space, and vitality for things that issue to you, more satisfaction, peace, isolation, rest and flexibility.

Include things you're enthusiastic about, things that enhance your life, significant connections, contributing past yourself to help other people, self-awareness, and learning, encounters and travel.

CHAPTER THREE
FOCUSING ON A SPECIFIC AREA THAT GIVES YOU THE SENSES OF ACCOMPLISHMENT

Rather than cleansing your entire system thoroughly, why not focus on significant areas at once. Take all things off it and independently evaluate what you will keep and what you want. Do likewise with different *expenses* of excess spending and unnecessary habits. Focusing on one particular precinct at any given moment will enable you to put more headspace into the procedure so you can settle on better choices and be more aware of your belonging which additionally causes you dispose of more things at once and forestalls inadvertently eliminating of vital elements.

Where you focus your attention decides your excited state. By focusing on your issues, you make and drag out negative feelings and stress, which impede execution. In any case, by focusing on activities to better yourself and your conditions, you can make a perception of personal adequacy that produces positive emotions and enhances execution. Fruitful minimalist individuals don't harp on issues since they realize that they're best when they focus.

Aristotle said this over 2,000 years prior. Regardless it continues till today. "What is the genuine reason forever, if not to carry on with a cheerful life until the point that we pass on?"

Satisfaction is a standout amongst the most looked for after objectives throughout everyday life, yet for some, it is by all accounts slippery. It's anything but complicated to hoodwink ourselves into considering, "When I simply have that pleasant house and new auto, at that point I can be glad." Pleasure is accessible to every one of us, at present.

The things that you don't take care of as it didn't exist, at any rate for you. Throughout the day, you are explicitly focusing on something, and substantially more frequently than you may associate, you can assume responsibility for this procedure to significant impact. Without a doubt, your capacity to focus on this and stifle that is the way to controlling your experience and, at last, your prosperity.

Living marginally is knotted with looking at life through reason – nature's most remarkable consecration to humanity. The significance of right in detecting and looking at life is apparent in all periods of life – from the baby who strains to investigate its new surroundings to the grandparent who effectively peruses and evaluates the features of the daily paper. Reason gives people a chance to take an interest throughout everyday life, to be human is to think, evaluate, and investigate the world, finding new wellsprings of real and otherworldly joy.

Our capacity to focus gives us a chance to achieve remarkable things – when it's functioning admirably. Diversions are the principle reason we lose focus, yet frequently these aren't as evident as you may envision. Instead, you may feel scattered or "fluffy," or reprimand yourself for not having more control.

As we get more seasoned, focus and fixation can change, as would memory be able to and other intellectual capacities which are, however, inescapable. Indeed, a few investigations with more seasoned individuals demonstrate no decrease in necessary leadership abilities, and the limit concerning crucial learning – utilizing particular strategies to comprehend something – can show signs of improvement with age. Individuals in their 70s can be "more principled and careful, without being hyper-watchful" than those in their 30s.

Having a weak focus may mainly cause you to invest more energy and resources into an additional project, and that system is most likely to cause you potential danger. Instead, you can have a better focus on making a move to advance upgrades in the particular cerebrum works that drive paranoia and mindfulness. By creating the conditions that make it less demanding to think and finish your job, you can feel keener and more focused when you have a particular errand to achieve.

We often yearn for new accomplishments since we rapidly habituate to what we've refined efficiently. This habituation to progress is as unavoidable as it is disappointing, and it's more capable than you understand.

The way to beating habituation is to seek after, what psychologists call – lasting achievements. Not at all like regular achievements that deliver short-lived bliss, the joy of persisting accomplishments keeps going long after that underlying buzz. Continuing achievements are critical to the point that they isolate the individuals who are fruitful and upbeat from the individuals who are left continuously needing more.

Asking yourself for the reason you need to might help you get a clear head. Is it accurate to say that you are attempting to alleviate the weight of a frivolous lifestyle? Do you need the quiet that accompanies a cleaned up space? It is safe to say that you are making space for huge dreams? When you require additional inspiration, recall that "why," perceive how far you've come, and focus on where you're going.

CHAPTER FOUR
PICKING WHAT STAYS AND WHAT GOES

Setting up a context to break down will dependably streamline your procedure. Take clothing, for instance, disposing of things you have not worn in the traverse of a year is a decent pointer. Connections that bring cynicism and disappointment rather than inspiration and joy ought to be given up. Settling markers for the different things will enable you to comprehend what you genuinely require with greater transparency. Just keep the stuff you need or see yourself lacking sooner rather than later – the rest ought to go.

From the minute we're conceived, we're advised to seek after surpluses. Notices from each TV, radio, daily paper, magazine, announcement, and site shout to us consistently. Accordingly, we buckle down hours with the goal that we can spend endless dollars obtaining the most exceptional homes, fanciest autos, trendiest designs, most prevalent toys, and coolest advances.

Be that as it may, we as a whole know it's not valid. We as a whole know, where it counts, that bliss cannot be purchased at a retail establishment– more isn't better. We've quite recently been told a lie such enormous numbers of times we start to trust it.

Imagine a scenario in which, in actuality, there is, in reality, more satisfaction in owning less.

That fact would change nearly every little thing about us. It would change the way we spend our hours, our vitality, and our cash. It would turn where we focus our consideration and our brains. It would change the very establishment of our lives. What's more, on the off chance that it was valid, it would free us up to seek after the things in life that we esteem. It would be an extraordinary and nurturing acknowledgment.

Sadly, for a few, the possibility of deliberately living with less belonging merely is too irrational. It's a way to deal with the life they have never been acquainted with or have never been welcome to investigate. The advantages have never been explained. Thus, it's too far a jump, too long an encompassing, so bouncing in with the two feet is only not going to happen.

Be that as it may, possibly there's a less demanding route than bouncing in wholly. Perhaps the way of life can directly be tested for a bit. One may not encounter every one of the advantages that are stood to the individuals who bounce in wholly. However, they just may taste enough to proceed with the journey into living a minimalist lifestyle.

You likely need lesser than what you think. We as a whole do. As you're choosing what to keep in your life, ask, "Would I be able to live without this?" If in this way, you know it's to a greater extent a need than a need. Demands need to remain. You get the opportunity to pick about the requirements.

Planning a basic life doesn't stop with your stuff. A more straightforward calendar can convey a wide range of peace to your days. Are there exercises you have to relinquish? Gatherings you don't have to go to? Dates to cross out? You realize what to do.

Certain frivolities consume the better part of income, and they are intended to pick up to be one after the other with a hundred percent hazard-free. Minimizing about three out of this life spending error with the instructions gotten from this book for about one month or so will give a decent vibe for the down to earth benefits, but hello!!!, it's your examination.

Outfits – As per well-researched insights, we wear 20% of our clothes 80% of the time. That implies that vast numbers of us have wardrobes loaded with garments that we never again like or never again fit us efficiently. They are merely consuming up the room. The first exercise of experiencing your wardrobe and evacuating all unused attire leaves your storeroom lighter, your mornings less unpleasant, and your closet brimming with things you adore. Give your lighter closet 30 days to work its enchantment; you'll never miss those unused wears.

A considerable lot of the embellishments in our homes hold no individual incentive to our lives. They just happened to coordinate the shade of the cover or be on special when we strolled into the store. Lamentably, they are diverting you and your visitors from the enhancements in your home that offer your story and feature your qualities. Pause for a minute to stroll through your home with a recognizing eye. Leave just the enhancements that are the most significant and the most wonderful. Your home will start to share your story flawlessly.

Toys – Time after time, we fall into the line of reasoning that says more is better thus do our children. We start to buy and gather dreadfully many toys for our kids. Therefore, our youngsters have no compelling reason to figure out how to be inventive, useful, watchful or sharing. In such manner, fewer toys may profit your children from numerous points of view. In spite of the fact that you might need to counsel your youngsters previously you migrate their unused toys, there's a decent shot that after just fourteen days the old, unused toys will be overlooked (except by whoever used to lift them all up).

Living and living expenses-. It might require some hard work, yet if you're up for the test, expelling copious furniture and other not that relevant property from your rooms will promptly open up large space and wind stream in your home. The once in a while utilized household items in your house are rapidly conspicuous and consuming up more room than you understand. Gracious beyond any doubt, this investigation requires a place to store your furniture amid the time for testing, yet it's a fast and straightforward approach to evacuate a portion of the most significant mess from your home.

Talk about the time and resources spent watching TV. Research has further proven that the average individual watches 4 hours, 35 minutes of TV every day. Furthermore, the average American home now has more TVs than individuals. There are 2.73 TV sets in the run of the mill home and 2.55 individuals. In an average house, a TV is turned on for more than 33% of the day. We are sitting on the love seat while life cruises us by. Explore different avenues regarding owning fewer TVs. Thus, you will observe less. Also, when you do, you will be more adept to do it together as a family.

There never is by all accounts enough space in our kitchens. However, the vast majority of our folks cooked significantly more frequently, substantially more intricately, and far superior than a large number of us today in appreciably smaller kitchens. In all actuality with regards to cooking, straightforward is quite often better. We require far less cooking utensils than we right now possess. At that point, store all your superfluous utensils in a plastic container put them away beyond anyone's ability to see, and check whether you merely appreciate cooking somewhat more in your new, mess-free condition.

Niches. The mess is a type of diversion. It pulls at our consideration and sidetracks our contemplations – notwithstanding for only a moment. Everything sitting out on your ledges goes after your attention. Shockingly, we have turned out to be so familiar with these digressions that we don't see them any longer, until the point of evacuation. Analysis, notwithstanding for only seven days, with keeping your ledges clear. Store things in drawers, cupboards, washrooms, or brief stockpiling boxes. Following one week, you'll likely restore some of it for comfort, yet I'd wager every last cent that you won't regain every last bit of it.

CHAPTER FIVE
PURCHASING BETTER

The best activity when adopting a reasonable strategy is to settle on buying less and utilizing current belonging more. In any case, when you do need to shop concentrate on adaptability and quality over amount. The most straightforward approach to forestall mess is to quit presenting pointless things that hoard the space.

What's more, no doubt about it, moderation is a choice. It is a decision to live counter-social. We have been advised since birth to devour and gather. Choosing to end up noticeably moderate reject those messages and purposefully picks less.

While life is loaded with choices, some of them are greater than others. Some of life's resolutions can be made without much discerning the future. Be that as it may, different choices ought to be made merely after the more significant part of the results have been considered. Getting to be noticeably moderate is one of those decisions – it isn't a choice to be gone into gently. While at first glance, moderation appears like merely discarding a bundle of messiness. It is a voyage that will at last end in your heart, psyche, and soul.

Owning things winds up noticeably essential when you have an inward void. At the point when your inside world is denied it is just average to need to fill it with outside things. Tragically, this resembles filling a sifter with sand. The sand may fit in the sifter incidentally, yet it will soon filter through the openings, abandoning you purge once more.

Consummation realism doesn't mean neglecting every one of your belonging. Freeing yourself of all that you claim would just demonstrate you are still excessively distracted with belonging themselves.

Somebody who has built up a substantial inward world would consider about be impartial. This move is more about state of mind than particular activities

The issue is that you see things as belonging in any case. Proprietorship is only a societal develop to keep and arrange; it doesn't have any more profound significance. Isolate your character from the things you claim.

Covetousness fills a void. Supplant that awkward filler with objectives and difficulties. Albeit a large number of challenges coordinated towards the material pick up, that isn't the original point.

The primary motivation to purchase a question is because you trust it will (straightforwardly or by implication) enhance the nature of your experience. Going straight to the source causes you maintain a strategic distance from the agents that are tangible products.

Streamline all your material belonging, so they don't devour your psychological assets. Basic, regardless of whether less captivating, requires less upkeep, offers fewer diversions and uses less reasoning. Minimalism bears you the capacity to concentrate your energies on your inward world.

CHAPTER SIX
FOLLOWING UP PERIODICALLY

Dole out a periodical follow up for each broad class and rehash the procedure to guarantee you remain jumble free. For instance, you can deal with your apparel at regular intervals or somewhere in the vicinity. Reassess and ponder your condition every once in a while to boost the utility of your physical and mental space.

Turning into a moderate can be helpful for some, particularly the individuals who are hoping to make a fresh start. It's a persistent procedure and some of the time requires facing and bringing an end to propensities that don't serve. It requires time and persistence, however, is regularly instantly advantageous.

The most definite advantage of having a more moderate way of life must have a cleaner home; less mess likens to less time cleaning. Less time is endeavoring to compose your things, less time cleaning and less time freezing because your home is a wreck when you have unforeseen visitors. Something I think we've all accomplished. Shouldn't something be said about other advantages? In spite of the fact that despite everything, you are dealing with limiting your expenses.

It can be useful to peruse about or see other individuals' variant of moderation to move and energize you all alone moderation travel. It's incredible to realize what is working for them and what hindrances they experienced en route.

We figure perceiving how other individuals "do" moderation is extraordinary compared to different approaches to take in more about fairness. It's an incredible method to move yourself to advance out of your usual range of familiarity and persuade yourself to explore living with less. In any case, you should make your particular form of moderation. One that works for your family, your way of life and your needs. Rather than merely attempting to duplicate another person's variant of restraint.

In any case, imagine a scenario where you are merely beginning on your moderation travel and are feeling overpowered without an arrangement of tenets or rules to take after. For sure if you've been cleaning up and limiting for some time, however, aren't sure how you'll know when you've achieved a position of enough in your variant of moderation?

With a little consideration and figured, you can make sense of what you need your form of moderation to resemble. Putting forth some necessary inquiries will enable you to get clear about what you need your rendition of restraint in parallel, and what you'll have to do to arrive.

Don't imagine it any other way; moderation is a choice. It is a decision to live counter-social. We have been advised since birth to expand and gather. Choosing to wind up noticeably moderate reject those messages and purposefully picks less.

While life is brimming with choices, some of them are greater than others. Some life's decisions can be made without much thinking ahead. Be that as it may, different verdicts ought to be made merely after the more significant part of the outcomes have been considered. Getting to be plainly moderate is one of those opportunities – it isn't a choice to be gone into softly. While at first glance, moderation appears like merely discarding a bundle of messiness. It is, indeed, a voyage that will at last end in your heart, psyche, and soul.

CHAPTER SEVEN
THE BENEFITS OF MINIMALISM

There are significant numbers of advantages to picking an average and essential life! Minimalism issue a decent way of life change for you if your living space influences you to feel intimidated, if you spend the dominant part of your day feeling surged, unfocused or restless, you have a feeling that you don't have sufficient energy to take part in exercises that influence you to feel invigorated and empowered, and in the event that you feel like there's insufficient time in the day to do everything.

Here is a portion of the advantages being a minimalist:

Additional Time – When you take out all that is pointless from your life (time responsibilities, abundance belonging, diversions), you have more opportunity to concentrate on and seek after what is imperative to you (your interests). Through disposing of unused and unneeded belonging, you free up time since you are investing less energy cleaning, keeping up, sorting out, inquiring about and looking for possession, repairing, and the sky is the limit from there. With this additional time, you would it be able to live at the time, interfacing with individuals and building your connections, developing and adapting new things, investing energy with family and companions, seeking after your interests and concentrating on your physical, mental and passionate wellbeing.

More Dynamism – When your opportunity is centered around doing things you're enthusiastic about rather than things that you despise, you will feel more empowered and invigorated.

More Freedom – When you have additional time, you likewise have more opportunity to invest your energy accomplishing a more significant amount of what you adore and what is important to you. When you have less belonging, you likewise feel lighter and more liberated to have the capacity to move around at whatever point you need.

More Money – Spending less cash purchasing new things, implies you are sparing more cash to spend on your interests, encounters, and voyages.

More Rest – When you have fewer time responsibilities and diversions throughout your life, you can set aside a few minutes for rest and unwinding, which are imperative to our physical prosperity.

More Delight and Joy – Joy originates from doing what you adore, being thankful for what you have in your life, and valuing the necessary things.

Greater Productivity – Focusing on one assignment at any given moment can cultivate expanded profitability and effectiveness. Single entrusting is superior to multi-entrusting.

Less Stress – When you have less real mess encompassing you and in this way, invest less energy cleaning, sorting out, looking for and keeping up your belonging, you will probably feel less focused and overpowered. Likewise, focusing on fewer things that take up your valuable time encourages you to explore less rushed and occupied.

More Space – More physical space in your home (from cleaning up belonging) prompts mental clearness too.

Furthermore, don't imagine it any other way, m is a choice. It is a decision to live counter-social. We have been advised since birth to devour and gather. Choosing to end up noticeably moderate reject those messages and purposefully picks less.

While life is loaded with choices, some of them are greater than others. Some of life's verdicts can be made without much planning. In any case, different decisions ought to be made merely after the more significant part of the results would be considered. Getting to be plainly moderate is one of those decisions – it isn't a choice to be gone into gently. While at first glance, moderation appears like merely discarding a group of messiness. It is, indeed, a trip that will eventually end in your heart, psyche, and soul.

The standards of minimalism will inevitably crawl into different parts of your life. You will soon start expelling trivial things somewhere else in your life. In the end, you will streamline your opportunity responsibilities, your objectives, your screen time, and perhaps your eating routine. A rearranged way of lifestreams typically out of a moderate way of life.

CONCLUSION

Thank you again for purchasing this book!

I hope this book was able to help you to satisfy your curiosity about the myths surrounding Minimalism and how to live happily with spending less.

The next step is to now is for you take charge concerning your sense of living with less spending and more productivity.

Finally, if you enjoyed this book, then I'd like to ask you for a favor, would you be kind enough to leave a review for this book? It'd be greatly appreciated!

Thank you and good luck!

www.ingramcontent.com/pod-product-compliance
Lightning Source LLC
Chambersburg PA
CBHW070950180426
43194CB00041B/2040